Learning by Doing Sociology

Learning by Doing Sociology In-Class Experiential Exercises

Linda Stoneall

University of Wisconsin, Whitewater

Allyn and Bacon

Boston • London • Toronto • Sydney • Tokyo • Singapore

Copyright © 1997 by Allyn & Bacon
A Viacom Company
160 Gould Street
Needham Heights, Massachusetts 02194

Internet: www.abacon.com
America Online: keyword: College Online

ISBN 0-205-19850-3

Printed in the United States of America

10 9 8 7 6 5 4 3 2   00

For Rose of Sharon & Lorna

Learning by Doing Sociology

Table of Contents

Preface

Learning by Doing Sociology shows how to teach sociology without just lecturing. It is the first book which joins several in-class exercises in one easy-to-use guide. The book offers general suggestions for managing experiential learning, step-by-step procedures for the activities, and trouble-shooting tips. With such a broad range of topics, professors have the flexibility to use all of the activities for general introductory social science courses, or to use the book as a reference to look up activities for more specialized courses, such as courses on race or gender.

Learning by Doing Sociology does not include experiential learning that sociology students engage in outside the classroom. The book also excludes computerized activities which require equipment currently not available to many classrooms. Interested professors can find both out-of-class exercises and computerized learning programs in *Teaching Sociology*.

Learning by Doing Sociology divides into two parts, general and then more specific advice on doing in-class exercises. Part One, General Guidance, offers an invitation to professors to reap the benefits of experiential learning. The second part, Specific Exercises, lists exercises with step-by-step procedures for executing the exercises.

The Birth of *Learning by Doing Sociology*

In 1982 I left academia for the business world of corporate training. Juxtaposition of two education extremes - lectures of academia and hands-on applications of training - taught me new possibilities in education. Whether the training was something as concrete as learning to run a machine or as abstract as leadership or something in between, like sales training, trainees did something. They tried out skills in the classroom before they performed those skills on the shop floor, office or clients' work place. The application of skills in the classroom allowed employees to increase their confidence with the techniques in a safe environment. Similarly, trainers could assess the extent of understanding and coach individuals to improve. Trying out the skills in training increased the possibility that employees would remember and use the tactics on the job.

After twelve years in corporate training, I returned to college teaching at the University of Wisconsin at Whitewater. There I was able to try uniting the abstract concepts of sociology with job training methods, and I created some exercises. Asking colleagues, looking in *Teaching Sociology* and the few books on college teaching yielded a few more activities. These exercises worked with large (50 student) freshmen classes as well as smaller upper class courses. *Learning by Doing Sociology* combines my efforts.

Acknowledgments

When I asked Greg Bell of Allyn-Bacon whether exercise books were available, he put me in touch with editor Karen Hanson who asked me to write a book. Thanks to Karen Hanson and Jennifer Jacobson of Allyn and Bacon for editorial assistance in carrying out the project. I also appreciate Steve Landfried, Charles Green and Mary Wilson for reviewing chapters. A special thanks goes to my students at the University of Wisconsin at Whitewater for trying out and actually liking the activities.

Learning by Doing Sociology

Part One
General Guidance

This section presents generalized teaching techniques for using exercises in class. The techniques apply across many types of exercises, many subjects and many types of classrooms. The first chapter defines experiential learning and argues the reasons for using experiential exercises. Evidence supports the benefits of learning by doing. However, the purpose of the book is not to convert disbelievers, but to show interested teachers how to lead students' activity within classrooms. Chapter 2 presents how to get students involved in many ways. Classroom management techniques not only include all students, but also avoid chaos and lack of learning.

Chapter 1

Why Experiential Learning?

Tell me and I'll forget.
Show me and I may remember.
Involve me and I'll understand.
                    Confucius

American university teaching has only recently begun to go beyond the first precept of Confucius' statement. Most professors profess and sustain the traditional lecture as the way to teach. The addition of films, video tapes, slides, diagrams and possibly symbols elevate classrooms to Confucius' second line. In both cases, telling and showing, students remain passive, empty vessels as lecturers pour out libations of knowledge. Confucius implies the vessel is more of a funnel, and the knowledge does not stick.

Involvement remains more of a puzzle, a dilemma, an unknown. When teachers ask for student involvement, students answer with silence. Does involvement depend on the personality of the teacher? Or are students at fault and lack motivation? Or are certain subjects, such as learning to drive a car, more amenable to involvement? I believe that some simple techniques can help both faculty members and learners engage in more active learning and that the subject of sociology is especially amenable to student involvement. *Learning by Doing Sociology* describes these techniques and how to do them in the college classroom.

What Does Active Involvement Mean?

Kolb calls student involvement in learning, experiential learning (1984). Others refer to involvement as participative or active learning. Bateman names the process, discovery (1990). Active involvement implies students do something, often something more kinetic than taking notes. Active involvement also branches out into collaborative learning (Cooper *et al.* 1994).

Lewis and Williams (1994) refer to John Dewey's philosophy of learning by doing and his book, *Experience and Education* (1947P) to describe the action: "For him [Dewey], experiential learning meant a cycle of 'trying' and 'undergoing' by becoming aware of a problem, getting an idea, trying out a response, experiencing the consequences and either confirming or modifying previous conceptions" (1994: 6). For sociology classes, students can generate, try out or apply sociological concepts. Students also work with each other, not only with the teacher.

Experiential learning takes advantage of the fact that students learn in different ways, and that each student learns in many ways. If professors use only one teaching technique, they do not reach all students or all the potential of any individual student. Kolb's research shows four basic learning styles common to everyone.

- Abstract
- Reflective
- Experimentation
- Concrete

In addition each individual specializes in a certain combination of these learning styles. Students apprehend information through abstraction and through concrete methods; they process information through reflective observation and active experimentation.

Abstract learning implies understanding broad concepts and theories. Most scholars have learned through abstraction, and most lectures appeal to this way of learning. Lectures also tap the reflective style of learning where the learner ponders on the meaning of ideas.

Even with these two styles, professors rarely give students a chance to do their own conceptualizing or reflection.

With the experimentation learning style, learners manipulate concepts and concrete objects to use theories to make decisions and solve problems. The last experiential learning style deals with concrete items, low level abstractions and actual things as students use them to discover broader ideas. Experimentation and experiential learning exist outside of lectures.

Readers will recognize that some learning styles involve deductive thinking, and others employ inductive thinking. In the learning-by-doing of this book, students may have already been exposed to broader ideas, through lectures and readings. Experience in the classroom can give students the opportunity to try out those ideas and apply them to different topics and examples. In other kinds of activities, students can discover and replicate many sociological ideas inductively, going from the concrete to the more abstract. Learners can then compare their findings to articles or texts that they read following their in-class experiments. Scheff (1992) and Bateman (1990) advocate discovery exclusively.

Variety

Using both deductive and inductive exercises not only appeals to different learning styles, but offers variety to students. Through variety, exercises not only overcome the number one complaint of young adults, boredom, but variety also stimulates several senses. Using more than one sense allows diverse repetition and increases the possibility that students internalize the ideas. The more senses learners use, the more likely students remember what they learned.

When the sense of sight combines with hearing (as in a lecture), comprehension and memory double. Adding the tactile sense of doing increases learning even more. Learning exercises reach students' affective and psychomotor ways of learning in addition to just the cognitive. While smell and taste are not included in this book, smelling and tasting could be welcomed additions to the study of culture and other topics.

At the minimal end of the range of involvement, students talk in addition to hearing and seeing. If students answer questions and express ideas in their own words rather than the professor answering and stating, students are starting to internalize the ideas. At the other extreme students may create and carry out an entire project from scratch. In this way, students are actually generating knowledge. Experiential learning can help students see the relevancy of social science, for example, for their own lives and careers because students themselves make first-hand discoveries using research methods instead of just reading about them.

Structures

In addition to the different learning styles and thinking processes, in-class learning varies in its structures, including the following types of organizations:

- Small groups
- Games
- Simulations
- Research methods

Many in-class exercises use small groups. The groups receive tasks or problems that they jointly carry out or solve. Sometimes called collaborative learning, such activities allow students to learn from one another.

Tannen (1990: 77) points out that small group discussions benefit female students more because as children, they play as more or less equals with small groups of friends. She suggests women converse to gain rapport and do not want to stand out. On the other hand, men value "report-talk," showing their independence and hierarchical social order, so they talk more readily in large groups. Combining large and small groups involves both female and male students at their optimum comfort level.

In another type of in-class activity, students play educational games. Many publishers sell board games or computerized games for learning social science, such as the Marriage Game (Greenblat, Stein and Washburne 1977) or SimSoc (Gamson 1978). *Simulation and Gaming in Social Science* (Inbar and Stoll 1972) suggest still more games. See Dorn (1989) for an excellent article on simulation games. *Learning by Doing Sociology* offers other games that teachers can set up on their own. For example, television game shows offer models relevant to classrooms.

Like games, simulations more directly let students approximate an experience which gives them a better understanding of theoretical concepts. For example, students can experience discrimination or class differences. The experience is not quite real since the professor contrives an in-class experiment. However, simulations mirror reality enough that students can observe and notice changes in behaviors and feelings.

Finally, research methods give students actual hands-on practice both to experience what sociologists do and to gather data to replicate or discover sociological ideas. Even with introductory or other non-research classes, students can experience the challenge and thrill of trying to observe, conduct a survey or interview right in the classroom.

In summary, with learning by doing, students actively participate in class and thereby not only process and internalize abstract ideas from readings and lectures, but also discover their own ideas. Student involvement entails many learning methods and several patterns of organization so that student activity taps multiple learning styles and appeals to students' desire for variety. Why don't more teachers use learning by doing instead of their exclusive employment of lectures?

Resistance to Experiential Learning

Objections to experiential learning include the following worries and unacknowledged fears:

- A preconception that experiential learning lowers academic standards

- Egotistical attachment to lectures

- Fear of the unknown

- Lack of control

- Too many students to involve all

- Not enough time for structured experiences

- Lack of skills and knowledge about experiential learning

Resistance even to films and videos derives from some professors' views that the methods regress to television watching instead of dealing with more difficult, abstract ideas. Such teachers might think: If students are actually doing something, isn't that akin to basket weaving? If students are playing games and having fun, how can they be learning? Should that kind of activity be a part of a rigorous education? Some professors think hands-on learning has no place in college and wastes students' time. The answer to the watering down fear is research that shows more retention with more action and less retention with lectures (see next section).

If students learn more and remember more with active involvement, then active learning produces more efficient results than lecturing. In-class exercises are not time-fillers for when professors have not prepared for class. Activities without learning objectives merely to entertain students would not be appropriate.

Not only might professors fear minimizing academic standards, but professors may think students will see the exercises as childish or that students won't cooperate. Contrary to thinking learning activities childish, students ask for more. Many students want to participate.

Bateman (1990) exhorts professors to let go of their egos. Since most professors learned through lectures, college teachers themselves continue the tradition, thinking if lectures worked for them, why not for all? Why change something that works? After all, many professors worked hard to put together lectures and organize all their learning for students, so why let go of their lectures? Many professors have information not found in books, and also many lecturers excel in organizing information from books.

The status of having more knowledge than students and showing that superior knowledge through lectures may motivate some teachers. According to Bateman, "Our job as teachers is not to preen our egos, even though preening is fun, but to prepare students to solve problems when we are no longer around" (1990: 25).

Fear of the unknown or lack of control may also inhibit professors from trying experiential learning. With lectures, professors know exactly how the class will proceed, and they prepare to fill the necessary time. It's true that change tends to be messy and chaotic. When students grapple with theories and methods, student involvement can appear out of control and unpredictable. Professors need some flexibility in experiential learning, but they can also plan and time the activities, as the other chapters in this book show.

Another mistaken belief is that student participation is possible only in small classes. All the activities presented in *Learning by Doing Sociology* occurred in classes of 50 or more students. McKinney and Graham-Buxton write about group activities in classes of 200 students (1993). Ingalesbee created a semester-long in-class project on communalism for a class of around 200 students (1992). Hamlin and Janssen (1987) divided large Introduction to Sociology classes into small groups to respond to videos.

Taking time away from lectures or covering the book is another complaint. If professors wish to impart all their knowledge or go over each reading assignment students receive, then that's all they may do. But if professors wish to provoke students to delve more deeply into subjects and examine them critically, then college teachers should work experiential learning into their curricula. As Cooper *et al.* point out, with increasing information, professors cannot cover everything anyway (1994: 85).

Misconceptions and fears summarize objections to veering away from lecturing from time to time. The following section gives evidence and further arguments that support experiential learning. To develop professors' skills in new methods of teaching, other chapters in this book relate specific techniques.

Benefits of Experiential Learning

The American Sociology Association recommends that "passive formats should be modified to include more inquiry through small-group exercises, case studies...and games...[These] provide training in the sociological perspective" (1991).

The activities force virtually all students to be active rather than doing homework, doodling or dozing while they're in class. Research shows that experiential learning offers more to students than traditional lectures. According to the latest research in cognition, students cannot merely receive information and repeat this information on tests to learn how to think. Instead, students must process or do something with the information in order to obtain knowledge (Resnick 1987). Critical evaluation, reformulation and transforming information all process information so that individuals "build extensive cognitive structures connecting the new ideas together" (King 1994: 16).

Rau and Heyl say, "Isolated students do not learn as much or as well as students who are embedded in a network of informal social relations" (1990: 144). According to Astin (1992), student's involvement with other students ties directly to measurements of learning, personal development, and satisfaction with college. Astin assessed over 200 colleges and universities to discover that interactions among students and students' interactions with teachers best predicted cognitive attitudinal changes.

Johnson *et al.* (1986) further correlate educational outcomes with learning groups. Johnson and Johnson (1991) assessed 193 studies of collaborative learning and found collaborative learning more effective than other types of teaching. According to Cooper *et al.*, "Retention rates for material that is presented in lecture and practiced in small groups is increased substantially" (1994: 85). Scheff (1992) adds that discovery learning increases the speed and depth of learning.

In-class exercises appeal to one of the excitements of teaching: changing people and seeing them learn. Professors can see immediately whether students grasp the information. Learners who are floundering or unable to answer some questions may need help. This method allows teachers to give individual attention, even with large classes, and Chapter 2 explains how this works.

Professors may frankly admit that this all sounds well and good, but they don't know how to do it. *Learning by Doing Sociology* answers many criticisms and inhibitions against using participative learning and shows professors how to reap the benefits.

What This Book Does for You

This book details how to set up classroom situations to inspire students' participation. Professors themselves can create an atmosphere of activity and involvement that makes students feel comfortable. The next chapter gives many suggestions that helps professors to manage classrooms. Teachers will learn how to set up groups, how to give directions, and what to do when students are in groups. Other guidelines suggest how to set up experiential classes from the very beginning and how to foster a participative atmosphere throughout the semester.

The remaining chapters offer specific learning activities, so professors need not devise the activities nor search through many references to find them. *Learning by Doing Sociology* will be the first to join several in-class exercises in one easy-to-use guide. The book suggests topics and situations for using exercises and step-by-step procedures for the activities. At the same time, teachers can customize the activities, individualize them for unique situations or use the exercises as models for creating their own activities.

To be most successful, professors need to prepare for experiential learning classes in a different way from preparing a lecture. Teachers should study the directions and make any desired modifications. Many of the exercises offer several alternatives for conducting the activity. Teachers' own creativity can only enhance the exercises. It is also recommended that professors visualize and rehearse exercises, mentally, if not a dry run. Then taking a deep breath plunges the daring teacher into doing it.

Each of the exercises have the following components:

- Background
- Objectives
- Topics
- Materials required
- Optional materials
- To Prepare
- Steps
- Discussion
- Problem
- Solution

First, a background section discusses the theories or concepts that inform the activity. This section tells how the activity relates to sociology. Some of the exercises are generic and have no specific reference to credit them. Second, objectives state what students should do and what they should get out of the learning. What performance outcomes reward the participants? The third part suggests topics relevant for the exercise. If any materials or preparation are required, they are listed in the next two to three sections: Materials Required, Optional Materials and To Prepare.

Steps list the procedure for the teacher to follow in carrying out the exercise. The list of procedures usually begins with directions for the class and includes objectives, what students should gain from doing the activity. The following step-by-step procedures tell teachers what should happen. The exercises should not take place in isolation, but teachers should guide students to make conclusions about the activity. Discussion questions help professors lead students to make connections and draw conclusions.

Learning by Doing Sociology anticipates difficulties in handling the exercises and tells how to handle problems. A section on problem solving offers suggestions for what could go wrong with the exercises and what professors can do to save the situation. Trouble-shooting tips allow teachers to use problems as learning opportunities.

With such a broad range of topics, professors have the flexibility to use all of the activities for general introductory social science courses, such as with Bryjak and Soroka (1994) or to use the book as a reference to look up activities for more specialized courses, such as a course on race or gender. The order of the exercises follow most sociology introductory topics.

Confucius' statement combines telling, showing and involving. Professors can continue to tell information or lecture to students, especially information that only professors themselves may have or that could be impossible for students to find out otherwise. Teachers should show students the many excellent videos, computer programs, and visual images.

I would like to challenge professors to take a risk and meet Confucius' appeal for student involvement. This chapter has presented many arguments on behalf of Confucius in the sociology classroom. Professors don't have to lecture, at least not all the time.

Those individuals who try experiential learning can supplement lectures with in-class exercises. Teachers can challenge students to delve deeper into the complexities of concepts, into the difficulty of collecting precise data, into the way sociology can apply to themselves. Why should professors have all the fun of researching and organizing information or creating theories? Teachers themselves may learn something new from their students.

Chapter 2

How to Manage Experiential Learning

Talking too much in class, or what might be called "linguistic rate-busting," upsets the normative arrangement of the classroom, and in the students' eyes, increases the probability of raising the professor's expectations vis-a-vis the participation of other students

Karp and Yoels (1976: 430).

For the brave individuals who decided to accept the challenge posed at the end of Chapter 1, Chapter 2 suggests how to manage students' activity in the classroom. This chapter provides some general guidelines, including help with some problems that Karp and Yoels' study raises.

Managing experiential learning means involving all students and not just the linguistic rate-busters. Maximizing students' learning experience in classrooms requires all students to participate and talk. Karp and Yoels' (1976) observations and surveys of students reveal unequal participation. A few students talk quite a bit more than other students. The surveys further show that other students dislike these few students who speak up, in part, because students who talk less fear they will have to talk more. In addition, students don't want to show their ignorance, their failure to read the assignment or their inability to formulate ideas.

Furthermore, Karp and Yoels suggest that "Students believe that they can tell very early in the semester whether or not a professor really wants class discussion" (1976: 424). If students think the professor doesn't really want discussion, they don't bother to discuss. In other words, students do not realize the benefits of their participation. Their fears outweigh any desires they may have to discuss a topic. This puts the initial burden on the professor. Early in the semester, from the first day, teachers can create a participative environment which inspires all students to speak up. This way, professors cannot blame students when, from time to time, teachers ask for participation and receive none or from only a few students.

This chapter shows many ways professors can plan for students to participate:

- Setting expectations

- Knowing students

- Remembering names

- Giving directions

- Organizing groups

- Leading discussions

Setting Expectations

It's important to let students know you want their participation, "I want everybody to say something." Sometimes you might have to repeat that message several times throughout the semester. A few professors may expect involvement from all, but fail to communicate that. Challenge students or suggest a quota or goal for them, such as one comment a week. Junn suggests giving three poker chips to each student each class and requiring all students to spend their chips on a comment, question or answer, but not more than that (1994: 147).

Beyond saying, "I want you to participate," putting that message in writing can reinforce the call for class participation. You can write your summons to participate in your syllabus or other handouts. For example, "This is a participative class. Every student should plan to answer one question or make one comment per class. This policy helps the class gain from the contributions of many people, and it will help you to remember the ideas." Create signs or messages on the blackboard that notify students you want them involved, such as the quote that began Chapter 1.

An even stronger reinforcement is to grade students for their participation. A certain proportion of students' final grade can be a separate class participation percentage or points. "15% of your grade is based on class participation." To a large extent, this is subjective, based on your observations.

A more objective way to include participation as part of the final grade is to keep a list of names and check each time a student makes a contribution. For some of the activities in this book, individuals or groups complete written work which can be evidence of their participation. Students could receive a grade or a pass-fail on the assignment.

Showing what you mean by involvement on the first class also lets students know what to expect. After they've had a chance to participate in an exercise, they can decide whether to stay with this section. The first-day exercise gets student and teacher acquainted.

Knowing Students

When you know your students personally, you can call on them by name and bring out individual contributions. Students feel more comfortable talking in class when they know other students. Also they are more likely to talk to fellow classmates and not just to the teacher, so that they learn from one another. Get-acquainted activities the very first day

of class serve a number of functions:

- Help you get to know students

- Let students get to know one another

- Make students feel more comfortable with the class

- Inspire students to speak in class and contribute to discussions

- Show students fun in the classroom

- Preview for students future types of activities

When students say something to the class the first day, they are more likely to say

something again. At a minimum, ask students each to state their names and beyond that,

introduce themselves further.

Dorn (1987) also advocates activities on the first day of class that transfer the class

from strangers to inter-connected people. Students need to know what the course and

instructor will be like (expectations). Dorn also suggests getting information on students

and learning their names. See Riffer (1983) for a first-class exercise using *Statistical

Abstracts*.

Many books delineate ice breakers (for example, Newstrom and Scannell 1980,

1991, 1994 or Forbess-Greene 1983), another word for get-acquainted exercises. Billison

(1986) applies small group theory to college classes and also mentions ice breakers. The

following paragraphs describe two exercises I have used and following that, I suggest

other ice breakers relevant to sociology classes. Besides familiarity with one another, the

purpose is to get all students to say something and ideally, relate what they say to the topic

of the class. Ice breakers introduce both people and subjects.

When I teach Individual and Society where I have 50 students, I ask students to

make two lists on 3 x 5 cards: characteristics about themselves as individuals and

characteristics about themselves that are social. In what ways are you an individual and in what ways are you social? Then I ask students to join another student whom they did not previously know, share their lists and asterisk which items they have in common. Next, each pair joins another pair to look for more commonalties and more introductions. Finally, I ask each group to choose one item which they share in common. As each group introduces themselves and their characteristic, I list the traits on the board under either individual or society. From there, I relate the class traits to the syllabus and how the readings and topics will tell them more about themselves.

When I teach Juvenile Delinquency with classes of only 30 students, I ask students in turn to introduce themselves and say what they think causes delinquency. Each subsequent student must repeat the names and opinions of all the preceding students. This exercise allows me to introduce the course and the theories it entails. Besides these two specific examples from my own experience, you can use other more general ice breakers and customize them to your own specific needs.

Ice Breakers with a Partner

As in the first example above, you can ask students to work with a partner. The following list suggests what the paired students can do.

• Undirected questioning

Ask students to get to know one other person. Then they could also introduce their partners to the class. Such an open-ended method lets students decide what they want to know about the other person.

• Use words from a provided list

Ask students to choose from a list of social science words - such as class, status, role, norm, culture, self, institution - to find out about their partners. Use the words to introduce the partner to the rest of the class or for large classes, to a group.

• Two truths and a lie

Indicate students are to tell 2 truths and a lie to their partner. The partner must guess which is the lie.

- What else are you?

   Students tell what they would be if they were something else - an animal, something to eat, a famous person, a book.

- Favorites

   Students tell their favorites - person, word, class, song.

   As in my example, the pairs can then join another pair to get to know two more classmates. That quartet could join others. Still larger groups could form. The same activities can work with groups. Other types of group ice breakers are games.

   Games

- Guess

   Pin or tape a word, concept, phrase or name on all or some students' backs, for example, Karl Marx. Students have to guess what their word is by asking others questions that give them clues. Students can proceed one at a time, or for larger classes, pin something on the backs of at least half the class members and let everyone mingle and give clues.

- Search for others with given traits

   Create a bingo card with various characteristics of people: play piano, lived in Florida, saw the latest football game, have lost a job, have been arrested, etc. Students must write a different name for each square by asking one another until they locate a different person for each square. The first to fill all squares wins. A treasure hunt is the same as bingo where students have to find people with certain characteristics.

   Whether the ice breaker is for two or a group, whether the ice breaker involves games or not, some sort of summary helps remind students why they engaged in the activity. It also is good to transition into another segment of the class.

Remember Names

The ice breakers tell you something about your students, and you may even remember a few names from the activity. To remember more of their names requires more work. The work is much like students' memorizing for tests. Memorizing keeps your neurons working and your brain cells connected.

Knowing names, above all, increases involvement. You'll have an easier time calling on people and bringing out the contribution individuals can make to the process. In turn, using students' names rewards them and increases the possibility of their repeat performance. Here are some ways to remember:

- Give students surveys so you have more information with the name.
- Give students 3x5 cards on which to write information about themselves.
- Ask students their names until you know the names.
- Write their names as they answer.
- Look at their names when they hand in tests or other written documents and associate the name with the face.
- Take notes on students when you learn information about them.
- Repeat a name you learn - either to yourself or to the student - at least three times.
- The first few periods, before class starts, walk around the room and name the students.

I often state part of my expectations as getting to know students' names. I apologize to them for having to repeatedly ask them. Students won't mind that you ask several times because they're pleased with your interest in them.

Setting expectations and getting acquainted happen during the first day of class. Getting to know names may take several classes, but soon you will know most students, if they attend and participate. Activities should continue throughout the semester. How you set up the activities is important.

Giving Directions

Whether an activity occurs the first day or later in the semester, the process runs more smoothly if you give good directions. You won't waste time with chaos or repeating explanations if students know exactly what to do and why. Explain what students are to do in terms of steps. Give examples, and if possible, demonstrate how activities are to proceed. For example, you could tell how you would respond, or if you don't want to bias student's responses, give a more generic example.

Tell why students are doing an exercise and what they should expect to gain from doing the exercise, unless you want them to discover something inductively. For example, in the naming groups or games mentioned above, I often discuss the business application of people knowing names to make more sales, network for new information or know their way around a company better. Keating (1987) argues for the need to give students purposes to overcome their alienation from class.

In addition to telling the directions, you might want to write directions - on the board or on a hand-out. If worksheets or other items accompany the exercise, go over handouts or objects and explain how to use them.

Another part of directions includes dividing students into pairs or teams. You'll need to tell them how to split up and where to go. You can ask students to help in the decision of grouping, but communicating what, how and where is important to prevent misunderstanding.

Organizing Groups

You can choose from many ways to divide classes for small group activities. Groups can vary in size from two up to ten or 15, depending on the activity. Five per group works well for including everyone in the small group in a discussion. The group members may be jointly working on an assignment. Aronson (1978) initiated the "Jigsaw," where each group member specializes in a part of the topic and teaches that part to the other group members.

Sometimes it is beneficial to keep the same groups over several periods, especially at first when students might feel more comfortable with others they already know. On the other hand, getting students involved with different people inspires cross-fertilization of new ideas. If the activity involves students observing other students, they might notice more about strangers than acquaintances.

- Let students put themselves in groups.

This method gives students a choice in the matter, but it can be chaotic. Some students might be too shy to join a group. In that case, you can assign just those shy students to a group. Students may go with the same people they always do, or just work with people sitting near them.

- By rows or columns

Ask all students within a row or line to work together. If you want the groups to be equal in number, you may have to trade until the groups match in size.

- By counting off

Decide how many groups you want and ask students to count off by that number. Point at students as they count to make sure they all are included. You can be creative and have them count off by the alphabet or by some string of facts you want learners to remember.

- Divide group members ahead of time.

Use the class roster and place students alphabetically or by some other characteristic, such as students' majors.

- Divide by characteristic

Sometimes you might want more homogeneous groups based on the topic at hand. For example, all people from cities, all people from small towns, all people from rural areas or all first borns, all youngest, all middle children. Physical characteristics, such as height, hair or eye color, or something like birth dates are other ways to divide groups.

At this point, students know what to do and they're in their groups. What should you do?

What to Do When Students Are in Groups

For many of the exercises, you are the leader and need to be directing the activity, such as saying things or asking questions. For activities where students are in small groups, that is not the time for you to take a break, talk to another teacher or discuss other topics with particular students. Rau and Heyl (1990) think it's best to leave students alone and not make them nervous, but I disagree. Instead, students working in groups gives professors an opportunity to give individual attention.

At first, get the groups going. Make sure everyone is in a group. If you asked class members to form partners, connect people who don't have a partner next to them. If groups seem to have difficulty starting, ask questions or make suggestions, often found in the problem-solving sections of the exercises listed.

Listen to and monitor groups. Is the group on the subject? Are students making progress? Learn from them new examples and ideas that you can throw back to the entire class. Use students' questions in the general discussion. Are all involved? Encourage reluctant learners who are not participating.

If a group is doing well, tell them so. If a group or individual is struggling, first get the group to see the problem and help each other. Sometimes it's appropriate to get another group or the rest of the class to help. Other times, you can offer suggestions that could go so far as helping the student or group outside of class.

Students can learn a lot from one another in groups. They are also struggling with ideas to make them their own. You are facilitating and guiding that learning. Further coaching of students comes in orchestrating summaries, connections and discoveries through discussion with the entire class.

Leading Discussions

Talking is a way to use language, learn new vocabulary and remember ideas and concepts. Discussions can extend to most, if not all of the class. Leading discussions requires good questions and orchestrating (see Stoneall 1991a; 1991b). Beyond factual questions, get students to think. Dillon (1988) suggests that less than 5% of teacher questions invoke a high level of cognition.

This section suggests ways to compose, ask and order questions. Ways to get students thinking and ways to get a wide variety of responses are other dynamics to leading discussions. This section also offers tips on dealing with problems, like the rate-busters in Karp and Yoels' study. Problems include one or more students dominating, belligerent or inappropriate comments and students who don't talk.

Questions reinforce readings, lectures and activities. Questions also lead students to discover new ideas. Questions almost stimulate in minds a vacuum that longs to be filled. When students answer in their own words, the ideas and concepts start to make more sense to them personally. Questions also drill and reinforce answers. Teachers can also use questions to assess students' understanding so teachers can speed ahead or look for other ways for students to deal with concepts.

If you're not used to leading discussions, it's a good idea to write out questions in preparation for discussions. I've included discussion questions for each activity, but you should put the questions into your own words.

How you arrange the classroom and yourself can impact discussions. If the class is small enough and the seats mobile, a U-shape or a circle gets all students facing one another so they are more likely to answer and question one another. If the professor sits at the students' level, this also lowers the power level of the professor to encourage more interaction among students, instead of just with the professor.

Again, I recommend asking questions from the first day of class to get students used to answering. An initial question that can get everyone involved is a polling question.

"How many of you - ?" Students raise their hands and everyone in the classroom can see who has answered similarly. For example, "How many of you want a career where you work with people?" Most students will raise their hands, so you can sell them on the study of sociology.

King argues that thought-provoking questions force students to connect, integrate and apply ideas (1994: 17). She lists types of thought-provoking questions including asking for examples, comparisons and contrasts, and evaluations (1994: 24). Hansen (1994) discusses taxonomies of questions ranging from clarification to analysis and synthesis, from classifying and sequencing to interpreting and predicting. Hansen cites Brophy and Good (1986) and Wilen and Clegg (1986) as evidence that class discussions enhance student learning.

For most discussions, open-ended questions work best because they inspire more elaborate answers. These questions begin with the journalists' Ws or H for how: who, what, where, when. Often it's better to precede the what before the why to make sure everyone shares a definition and references the same idea. From agreement on definitions, you can go into causes, origins and consequences. For example, "What's a norm?" then, "Why do societies have norms?"

Close-ended questions often begin with "Is - ?" or "Are-" and lead to yes or no answers. Close-ended questions tend to discourage discussion. For example, students rarely answer the question, "Are there any questions?" It's better to ask, "What questions do you have?" because that more clearly communicates that you want questions.

Sometimes stopping a discussion could be appropriate, such as at the end of the class. Occasionally, you might want to ask leading questions which imitate Socrates: "Isn't it true that -?" For example, from *Phaedo*:

> When a thing becomes bigger, it must...have been smaller first before it became bigger?

Yes.
And similarly, it must be bigger first and become smaller afterward?
That is so...
And the weaker comes from the stronger and the faster from the slower?
Certainly.
...If a thing becomes worse, is it not from being better? And if more just,
from being more unjust?
Of course.
Are we satisfied, then, said Socrates, that everything is generated in this
way - opposites from opposites? (Plato 1961: 53).

Asking students to agree with a series of steps in an argument leads them to accept the

conclusion, but questioning with close-ended questions reverts back to the teacher doing

the talking and not the students.

Avoid the process of professor definition followed by a question about the

definition. For example, don't say, "A norm is a rule of conduct. What is a norm?" Careful

wording of questions can prevent the undesired game of "guess what's in the professor's

mind," such as, "What did Durkheim really mean by that?"

For each class, if you ask opinion questions first that have no right or wrong

answer, students will feel more comfortable. Don't take just one answer. Ask another

student if he agrees with the first. "What do you think of what she said?" "Who disagrees?"

Proceed to asking for definitions of concepts, examples of the concepts, and other

applications of the ideas. Invite others to elaborate or state alternative positions so students

are engaged with one another as well as with the teacher. Similarly, when students ask

questions, don't answer them so easily yourself. Turn the questions back to the class and

ask students to answer the student question.

When you first ask a question, ask it to everyone in general. If you say a name or

point to someone and then ask the question, no one else even needs to think about the

question or answer. Then either ask for volunteers or call on specific individuals or groups.

What if no one answers? After you ask, wait. Silence encourages thinking. Silence

can feel uncomfortable to professors not used to it. Maintain eye contact and look around, expecting the best answer from each student. If you're very uncomfortable, you might try counting silently to yourself. The discomfort of silence also entices students to fill in the void.

After a silence has still not led to an answer, repeat or rephrase the question. Ask a student to state the question. One way for you to rephrase a question is to narrow the possible answers and to give alternatives: "Is it this or that?" Call on someone by name as a last resort. Occasionally you might want to directly address the fact that no one in the class knows the answer and perhaps explore why. Such a discussion can help students learn how to learn.

Giving feedback on answers reinforces answers and gets students to answer again. Bateman disagrees and says teachers ought to create tension by not revealing whether the answer is right or wrong or whether the teacher agrees or disagrees. "Don't you dare tell that student that the answer is right. Don't you dare deny the class the fun of thinking and deciding and judging" (1990:183).

I like to praise learners' answers. It is not necessary for the teacher to respond to every answer, but smiling, nodding and saying, "Good answer," inspire students to talk more. What if the answer is wrong?

Bateman sends students to the library or elsewhere to bring in evidence about their answer. I ask the class if they disagree. Also, if part of the answer is correct, let the student know.

Problems in discussions

In just about every class some students dominate discussions and others do not say a word. Karp and Yoels were right about the rate-busters. Again, establish the ground rules in the beginning that all participate. Small groups with specific assignments force all to participate. In larger groups, if a few people dominate, talk to them outside of the class. Thank dominant talkers for their comments and ask them to let others have a chance. Give talkative students a quota of one comment per week or per class. See Junn's suggestion of poker chips (page 15-16 of this chapter). Tell them you'll call on them if no one else knows the answer. Sometimes, you can give these eager students additional ways to help in class, such as writing on the board or running video or slide equipment. It's easy to let the same few people talk all the time, so teachers need to make a conscious effort to involve others.

Sometimes the talkative student gets off the subject and occasionally such meanderings can lead to new insights. Other times, the irrelevant talk may make other students feel they are wasting their time. Interrupt the off-the-subject student by saying something positive about the diatribe. Then ask another question to the rest of the class. Use body language to show you are addressing the question to others and not to the talkative student.

If a student wants to argue in a non-academic way that puts down the teacher, or worse, another student, again the professor must intervene. Suggest that the student talk to you outside of class and then proceed with other questions. Part of your job is to educate students how to dialogue by not allowing belligerency in class and coaching other behaviors with the individual.

What about those who don't speak? Their good ideas could be lost and the opportunity for them to learn more foregone if they remain silent. Announce that you're going to call on those who haven't said anything since you know they have good ideas. Ask the question first, then call on students by name. Soon, many of them will be regular participants. Others will probably participate in the small groups.

In sum, leading discussions requires much thinking on your feet and spontaneously composing new questions. Practice can perfect the art of discussion leading that gets students learning more than if they remain silent. Whether discussion is the only activity or a follow-up to another activity, it is important.

Setting up expectations, coaching students throughout the semester and eventually calling on all students can avoid the linguistic rate-busting that Karp and Yoels observed. When all students start to feel comfortable with dialogues, rate-busters fade away. Students' dislike of the rate-busters also disappear, so students enjoy classes better and are open to learning more.

Part Two
Specific Exercises

The exercises in this section offer professors many choices. You can use them as they are. You can apply them to new or additional materials or subjects. Finally, you can use them as models for creating your own alternative activities. The exercises all get students doing something, often with other students. In this way, students experience ideas in a variety of ways and thereby internalize concepts.

Each exercise leads you from beginning to end: how to set up the exercise, hone students' knowledge and skills, and finally discussion questions, to make activities relevant to both the concepts and to students' lives. If you need materials, the section lists them and may even offer worksheets. The order of the exercises tends to follow the order of most introduction to sociology books, from methods to theory, from micro to macro sociological issues.

The Problem Solving sections with each exercise hint at detours students might take in the exercises. Almost all the so-called problems are actually opportunities that illustrate the point of the exercise and provide you with a way to guide students' discovery of sociology. Use problems as data to illustrate theories and methods. Other problems have to do with students' lack of understanding. Here, the opportunity is to individuate teaching and even let classmates provide alternative explanations and ways of looking at society.

Chapter 3
Break a Norm

Background

Norms, those everyday rules that control people, form a major building block in sociological theories. Breaking norms makes students more aware of the existence of norms. Garfinkel (1967) who studies taken-for-grantedness in everyday life, gives examples of norm-breaking. Garfinkel set up many experiments such as students acting like guests in their parents' home or riding elevators backwards. Students can create their own experiments that they can do during class.

Objectives

Students break a norm to understand norms and sanctions.

Topics

Introduction to Sociology

Norms and sanctions

Deviance

Experiments

Ethnomethodology

Materials required

None

Steps:

1. Explain that students are to devise an experiment to break a norm, like one of Garfinkel's experiments. For example, ride the elevator backwards to show norms of riding an elevator facing the door, not

showing eye contact. If possible, students should carry out the experiment or else imagine what would happen if they did carry it out. Caution them not to do anything that would harm someone or that is illegal.

a. Choose a norm to break.

b. Strategize how you'll do it.

c. Do it!

d. Notice the reactions of others

2. Divide the class into groups of 5-8 people.

3. Get them started.

4. Proceed until each group has carried out the experiment.

Discuss

1. What norms were broken?

2. Why did some students not actually break the norm?

3. What did others feel and think about the norm-breaking?

4. What responses occur when people break norms? List these on the board.

6. How can we categorize the types of norms, based on the experiments?

7. What do you conclude about norms and social control?

Problem-solve

Problem

Some students don't carry out the experiment. They devise an experiment to break a norm, but they don't actually do it.

Solution

Point out that disobeying the teacher does break a norm. Use their examples to discuss embarrassment and other feelings about why people don't break norms. Help them to see that social norms control them.

Problem

Students leave class to break a norm.

Solution

Use the action as a good example and point out others could have thought of that too.

Chapter 4

Scientific Problems

Background

Scientific problem statements pose questions, usually based on theories and propositions that a social scientist wants to research. Concepts, which are abstract words and phrases, form propositions. In turn, problem statements lead to hypotheses, specific connections of concepts to be tested. In order to make concepts testable, researchers must define them in a measurable way, the operational definition.

Objectives

Students write problem statements, operational definitions and hypotheses to grasp the way to translate theories into concrete research.

Topics

Methods

Materials required

Worksheet

To Prepare

Introduce students to scientific methods via readings or lectures.

Steps:

1. Explain that groups are to answer the questions on the worksheet. Go over the questions and give examples:

   - topic - suicide
   - concept - religion

- operational definition - on a questionnaire, subject checks membership in a particular sect

- problem statement - What is the relation between suicide and religion?

- hypothesis - Protestants have higher suicide rates than Catholics.

2. Allow about 20 minutes for them to complete the worksheet.

Discuss

1. Take each question and ask several groups what they decided.

2. Ask other groups to say what was good and how they would improve each problem statement, operational definition and hypothesis.

Problem-solve

Problem

Students can't choose a topic.

Solution

This problem might happen because students aren't yet familiar enough with sociology or because the group can't reach consensus. Offer suggestions, for example, turn to the Table of Contents in an Introductory text. Suggest they go along with their interests. As a last resort, get them to use Durkheim's suicide (1951) or some other model they've seen.

Problem

Students can't figure out concepts, operational definitions, problem statements or hypotheses.

Solution

Ask another group who does understand to explain.

Offer additional examples.

Scientific Problem

Names of people in group:

As a group, decide and write the following:

1.   Choose a topic. If you can't decide, use Suicide (ala Durkheim).

2.   Choose at least 3 concepts within that topic. Choose more concepts if you have time.

3.   Write an operational definition for each concept.

4.   Write a sociological, scientific problem statement for that topic. Write it in the form of a question, such as "What is the relationship between age and suicide?"

5.   Write at least 1 hypothesis on this problem. Indicate which is the dependent and which is the independent variable. (See Durkheim's example on age and suicide.) Write more hypotheses if you have time.

Chapter 5

Take a Survey

Background

Many classical surveys form the basis of theories and concepts. When students take the surveys themselves, they gain understanding of the source of the theories. They can also get practice in analyzing surveys. The analysis of their particular class may give them thought for criticizing or updating the original theory.

Objectives

Students take and analyze a survey to learn how to write surveys and to understand evidence that supports theories.

Topics

Methods

Topics associated with classical surveys

Materials required

Copies of the surveys

To Prepare

- Assign readings on survey construction or on the topic of the particular survey.
- Choose and copy the surveys. The example below is with the topic of discrimination and the survey is part of Adorno's Authoritarian Personality (1950).
- For the second class period, make copies of the answers.

Steps:

1. Distribute the surveys.

2. After students take them, ask for their ideas for analyzing the class surveys.

3. At the next class period, explain that groups will analyze the suvey questions. Each group will decide how to count and show the results and then present to the class.

4. Divide the class into groups of 4-6 students. Assign different questions to each group.

5. Allow at least 30 minutes, more if students need it.

6. Ask each group to report the results and make a tabulation of the total responses from the class, for example 55% females, 45% males.

Discuss

1. What did you notice about the questions? What kinds of things did they ask? How were they worded and formatted?

2. Do you think the questions measured the concept? What is an operational measurement?

3. What ways did you use to analyze the data? What makes it consistent and objective?

4. How could we check for validity and reliability?

5. What can we conclude about the results for this class?

6. How do the results compare to the original study?

7. Why are there differences or why are they the same?

Problem-solve

Problem

Students experience difficulty taking the survey.

Solution

Help individuals understand the questions. If many students have difficulty, use their difficulty to lead the class in critiquing surveys. Help them see the need to word surveys carefully and pre-test.

Problem

Adorno or other surveys are out of date and no longer apply.

Solution

Ask students to rewrite out-dated questions and make the questions relevant.

Problem

Students experience difficulty analyzing survey questions.

Solution

Unless this exercise is for a methods class or for students who have statistics, keep the analysis simple. Ask students to do frequency counts and/or percents. Go over examples of how to do counts and percents. Ask others in the class to help the struggling group.

Chapter 6

Write a Survey

Background

Questionnaire writing is one of the main data-collecting skills in sociology. Sociologists conduct surveys to reach a large number of respondents, to be able to categorize responses and to test hypotheses. Students can not only understand survey methods, but also get examples from their classmates of particular concepts when they write and give surveys. In addition to writing surveys, analyzing them also provides first hand experience with the difficulties and nuances of surveys.

Objectives

Students write and analyze a survey to appreciate and develop skills applicable to research.

Topics

Methods

Other topics

Materials required

Worksheet, such as example

To Prepare

Choose a topic. The example given below is to create a survey about religious beliefs and practices in the class.

Students should have read or heard about surveys previously.

Steps:

1. Explain that students will write survey questions. For example, check which sect best describes your current church membership:

Protestantism

Catholicism

Judaism

Other _____

None

2. Divide the class into groups of 3-5 students.

3. Students write survey questions.

4. Then each group answers another group's survey.

5. The group that wrote the questions, analyzes the answers.

Discuss

1. What are examples of questions?

2. What did you learn about the best way to write the questions?

3. Why do researchers pre-test questionnaires?

4. What is the benefit of using questionnaires for a topic like religious practices?

5. What do the results say about religious practices among people in the class?

6. How generalizable are the results? How could we make them generalizable to the campus as a whole? to the state? to the United States?

7. How do the results compare to what you read and heard about religions practices in this country?

Problem-solve

Problem

Poorly constructed questionnaires

Solution

Approve questionnaires before the class tries to answer them. Ask questions to get the group to improve their own surveys. Alternatively, lead the whole class in analyzing and critiquing questions without revealing which group wrote them.

Sociological Methods

Questionnaires

Names of people in group:

1. Choose topics based on the readings about religious practices in the United States. List the concepts below:

2. Decide who you would survey, that is, what kinds of people?

3. How would you distribute the questionnaire? Mail or in person? Why?

4. Write 5-10 survey questions on your topic. The first questions must
be multiple choice. The last one can be more open-ended.

Chapter 7

Interviews

Background

> Sociologists interview subjects to generate hypotheses, collect life histories and discover unexpected information. Interviews may also accompany observation methods. Interviewing classmates gives students an appreciation of the vagaries of interviews. Devising interview questions further shows them the need to word questions properly. Just about any topic is amenable to interviews.

Objectives

> Students create interview questions, then interview a partner to understand how to interview and to learn more about a specific concept or theory.

Topics

> Methods
>
> Any topic

Materials required

> Possibly worksheets, as the example given.

To Prepare

> - Decide topic, as in the example below, interviews were used in conjunction with a chapter on educational institutions.
> - Assign readings or lectures on interviewing or on the topic at hand.

Steps:

1. Ask students to think of the concepts in the book on what education does for people, both from a functionalist and a conflict viewpoint. For

example, socialization. Then write a question, for example, what did you learn in school besides the subjects and book learning?

2. Students write at least five questions based on the concepts.

3. Students interview a partner and record the answers.

Discuss

1. What questions did you write? What concepts do they relate to?

2. How could your questions be improved?

3. What is a topic you think most people asked about? List answers from this question so the class can generalize.

4. What would you need to do to make the interviews representative?

5. How could you analyze the answers to questions?

6. What problems do you see in interview data?

Problem-solve

Problem

- Student can't think of questions.

- Poor wording of questions

- Unethical or inappropriate questions

- Student can't get partner to answer.

Solution

Any misunderstanding of interview question writing can be an occasion for individual help or getting classmates to help. Find out exactly what the problem is and then why the problem is happening. Analysis of the problem should guide you in how to help the individual. You can ask questions and refer to examples. Lead the whole class in a discussion on how to improve wording and how to get people talking.

Interview Worksheet

Your name:

Based on the concepts from the book on the functions of education, write 5 interview questions below.

Then interview your partner. List your questions and answers to the interview below:

1.

2.

3.

4.

5.

Chapter 8
Content Analysis

Background

In *Gender Advertisements* (1979), Goffman showed how ads portray females differently than males. Studies of documents and records such as historical letters or even field notes analysis relies on content analysis. Students can do content analysis in a class to learn about gender or other issues.

Objectives

Students analyze magazines or newspapers to determine categories, count the frequency of categories and draw conclusions or hypotheses.

Topics

Gender

Minorities

Methods - Content Analysis

Materials required

Magazines and/or newspapers, students can bring

Optional materials

Goffman's pictures

Worksheet

To prepare

- Gather enough magazines or newspapers to have two or more per group.

- Or, a few class periods ahead of time, ask students to bring them to class.

• Prepare an example to show, such as the position to the viewer of females vs. males and their eye contact in ads in a movie magazine.

Steps:

1. Give instructions that students are to do the following:

• First, look through magazines or newspapers to get ideas for categories.

• Choose 1-2 categories.

• Make the counts.

• Create a table that shows the counts.

• Write a conclusion.

2. Go through your example. Show 2-3 pictures that illustrate something like position or eye contact. Show how the counts illustrate gender difference and what conclusion you could make.

3. Divide the class into groups of 5-8 students per group.

4. Get them started choosing one or two periodicals and paging through to decide categories.

Discuss

1. What did you discover? Call on each group until the findings seem to repeat.

2. Ask the class as a whole to come up with some generalizations or hypotheses.

3. What were the problems with this method?

4. What benefits are there to this method?

5. How else could you use the method?

Problem-solve

Problem

Students can't decide which materials or which categories to use.

Solution

Ask questions to find out their interests. Push them to choose.

Problem

Students have difficulty in determining the category of a particular picture or article because it is ambiguous or overlapping more than one category.

Solution

Take a poll of the group to determine how to categorize. Use the example to point out problems are part of any content analysis and the ways social scientists have handled it: throw out that piece of data or look for agreement among analysts.

Problem

Students didn't bring newspapers or magazines.

Solution

Have extras available. Use the student newspaper.

Chapter 9

Library Research

Background

Not only is the library a place to create a bibliography, but it is also the location of government documents and other reference materials Here, students can find rates, distributions and other already collected data. Many topics lend themselves to library research. This can be done as individual or group activities during class. It helps when students have some worksheet to guide them.

Objectives

Students look up information on particular topics to become more familiar with locating information.

Topics

Any

Materials required

Worksheet

To Prepare

- If necessary, obtain permission of the library to bring in the class.
- Ascertain the location of data and the years of volumes available.
- Decide topic and how to divide class.
- Create worksheets. The example below uses the Uniform Crime Report.

Steps:

1. Explain that students are going to learn first-hand what is in the Uniform Crime Report. They can use this information for reports, to look up statistics or they may need it on a job.

2. Have students count off to form groups.

3. Give a worksheet to each group.

4. Take the group to the library.

5. Show them the location of the Uniform Crime Reports.

6. Assign a different volume to each group, starting with the most recent.

Discuss

1. Go over each question with different answers from different groups.

2. Why are there differences?

3. What did you discover?

4. How would you use this again?

Problem-solve

Problem

Volumes are missing or being used by someone outside of the class.

Solution

Reassign group to different volumes.

Problem

Students can't find answers from worksheets, either because not all volumes have the same data or because the information is not easily organized.

Solution

Encourage students to continue looking. If they still can't find data, page through and offer suggestions. Note ahead of time which volumes lack certain data.

Uniform Crime Report
Worksheet

Group member's names:

Volume number:

What does the crime clock tell you?

Who are most likely to be victims of violent crimes? (sex, age, race)

What weapon was used the most?

What are different types of robbery? Which is the most frequent?

What are different types of larceny? Which is the most common?

In [your state], what is the violent crime rate?
What is the property crime rate?
Which violent crime had the highest rate?
Which property crime had the highest rate?

What percentage of people in [largest city in your state] were arrested for murder compared to how many were arrested in [your region of the nation]? How many murders were in [your college town]?

List 5 other types of statistics from the report that interest you:

Chapter 10

Role Play

Background

Symbolic interaction develops the concepts of role taking and role playing (Mead 1934). Role-taking refers to putting yourself in someone else's place. When students role-play, they take on a part, act like someone else. Role plays can be of specific people, for example Max Weber. Or students can represent people of different classes, different races and ethnic groups, different genders, different lifestyles, different positions within institutions.

Objectives

Students state reactions to issues according to various theorists to put themselves in the place of a theorist.

Topics

Theory

Social Psychology

Symbolic Interaction

Various

Materials required

None

To Prepare

- Choose a topic or topics for role-players to react to, such as a current event, a social problem or social science concepts.

- Choose a format for them to role play such as with partners, debate, or news cast. In this case, a news panel discussion, like

"Meet the Press," is the format. In this example, students role-play theorists.

- (Optional) Find a costume to dress like an historical figure.

Steps:

1. Designate individuals or groups as specific theorists such as Marx, Durkheim, Weber, C. Wright Mills, Goffman, G.H. Mead, Cooley, Simmel, Toennies, Wirth, Kuhn, Davis and Moore, DuBois, M. Mead, R. Benedict, Bernard, Parsons, Merton.

Note: With large classes where you assign groups to a single theorist, you can either repeat the role plays several times, ask them to take turns with different aspects of the theory, or ask the group to choose one role-player whom the rest of the group coaches.

2. Tell the individuals or groups to prepare to respond to current welfare policies as that theorist would if she or he were here today. For example, if you were Freud, you might discuss how civilization is trying to put restrictions on people or regress them to a dependent state.

3. Give them time to prepare.

4. Call various role-players in a panel of 5 people.

5. Ask each theorist to present their interpretations of current welfare policies.

6. Ask panel members to argue with or refute one anothers' positions.

Discuss

1. How can we summarize the gist of each theory?

2. Which theory gives the best explanation?

3. What kinds of testing would we need to do to compare the theories further?

4. Which theories would lead to the elimination of welfare?

5. Which theories would radically change welfare?

6. Which theories would like the way welfare is today?

Problem-solve

Problem

Student doesn't accurately represent theorist.

Solution

Coach individual students during their preparation to help them

understand.

Chapter 11

Impression Management

Background

Goffman (1959) discusses what kinds of things people notice about one another when they first come into each other's presence. He goes on to use the concepts of expressions given and expressions given-off which people can use to determine truth and the extent of control over the situation the other is exerting. Body language composes most of impressions and expressions, and students can become more aware of non-verbal communication.

Objectives

Students list their observations and impressions of a stranger to concretize Goffman's ideas.

Topics

Social Psychology

Symbolic Interaction

Communication

Non-verbals

Participant Observation

Gender

Materials required

Handout to guide observations (optional)

To Prepare

Assign readings from Goffman.

Decide whom students will observe. It should be someone they don't know:

- Bring in a stranger.

- Use a videotape, without sound.

- Ask students to pair up with someone in the class they don't know well.

Steps:

1. Explain that students will be observing a stranger and listing all their objective observations, then listing their interpretations or impressions. For example, notice teacher wears jeans. Impression: trying to appear younger, more hip.

   Optional: ask partners to tell a lie to see how they manage it.

2. Divide class or bring in video or person. I pair females with males.

3. Get them started.

Discuss

1. Elicit many observations from students and list them on board or overhead. What did you observe?

2. Which are objective and which contain judgments or impressions?

3. How can we categorize the observations: clothing, hair, posture, gesture?

4. Take some of the common observations and ask for interpretations.

5. How was the other person trying to control what you think of them?

6. What did you observe that revealed something behind the facade of the person?

7. How do your observations relate to Goffman or other readings?

Problem-solve

Problem

Reluctance or fear to work with a stranger and take notes on that person, particularly someone of the opposite sex.

Solution

Encourage partners to do it.

During the whole class discussion, acknowledge the discomfort.

Point out the difficulties of doing research, the difference between

covert and overt participant observation, the way to take notes.

Also, use the problem to bring out other aspects of impression

management. You're not supposed to note someone doing it. People

don't like calling attention to impression management, and

impression management implies no meta communication. That is, a

tenet of impression management is not to talk about it.

Impression Management Worksheet

Directions: Observe a partner. Record the expressions you notice. How do you interpret them?

Expressions Given-Off	Impression

Chapter 12
Group Dynamics

Background

Bales' (1966) experiments show different roles and positions of group members within a small aggregate. Teams of observers watch a group in action directly, through a one-way mirror or on video. Businesses use this technique for hiring, promotions and other decisions about employees. Businesses also use focus groups to improve advertising, product mix and general business practices.

Objectives

Students observe interactions within groups using a check sheet to practice observation in action.

Topics

Groups

Statuses

Roles

Leadership

Gender

Observation

Materials required

Check sheet

To prepare

1. Create check sheets, or use the one given or have the class create them.

2. Decide a topic or task for group participation. It's a good idea for this exercise to involve consensus decision-making. Survival kinds of activities work best for this. Suggestions:

- Ship wrecked on a tropical island, on another planet, afloat in the ocean with given list of provisions, what will they use? How will they use it? (provisions: matches, rain coats, newspaper, compass, 1 gallon of water, gun, survival book, mirror, etc.)

- Plane wrecked in a desert, in a jungle, in a snow storm, how will they use just what they have in their pockets and bags?

- Only one person can get medical treatment, given a list of types of people, whom do they choose? (types of people: newborn, famous person, expecting mother, 90 year old, dying scientist on the verge of discovering cancer cure, etc.)

Steps:

1. Explain that the class is going to observe a group to discover how groups work.

2. Ask for volunteers who aren't afraid to speak in front of others.

3. Choose 3 female and 3 male volunteers. If possible, also include minorities.

4. Ask the volunteers to leave the room so they can't hear.

5. Ask the remaining students, the observers, to form one large circle.

6. Give them the observation sheets.

7. Briefly explain how to observe, by ticking off each time they observe one of the actions. Explain and give examples of each item they are to observe. Tell them that they cannot talk to the small group or to one another during the small group discussion. **If you use the given observation sheet,** alert the observers to be prepared to record which person talks first.

As an alternative, assign observers to individuals in the group.

8. Bring the volunteers back into the room to sit in a small circle inside the larger circle.

9. Ask the large group to record the names of the participants in the small group as you name each one.

10. Explain to the small group what they are to discuss. If you are using instruction sheets, give them the sheets.

11. Tell the group to start.

12. Stop the group when they have come to a final decision.

13. Ask the large group to add up their tallies.

14. Ask both groups to write answers to questions about groups.

Discuss

1. Ask the small group the observation check sheet questions and then ask the larger group. Discuss why the groups differ in observations and why the disagreement occurred among the larger group members.

2. If appropriate, ask them to relate the exercise to readings or lectures on groups.

Problem-solve

Problem

- Observers can't keep up with the small group interaction and record all the dynamics.
- Tallies differ.
- Small group and large group don't agree on what happened.

Solution

All these problems actually yield learning opportunities. Because students usually can't keep tallies on all six members of the small group, they discover how rapid and complex interactions are. Even assigning observers to specific small group members shows observers that it's difficult to see where one interaction ends and another begins.

A similar process goes on with differences among tallies. The existence of differences can lead to a discussion of validity and precision in the social sciences. Students can brain-storm ways to make counts more accurate such as videotaping.

When the small group members aren't sure or disagree among themselves, observers learn that participants in a group are not always self-aware. This shows additional information about group participation. Observers see the benefit of stepping back and developing a framework for observing.

In sum, as a result of problems in this exercise, students develop a better appreciation of collecting social data.

Groups
Observation Sheet

Your Name:

You will be observing a discussion group. As you observe, take notes on the following:

List the people in the group in the first column. Put a check mark for each occurrence in the

other columns.

Name	Talks first (one check only)	Talks	Initiates a sug-gestion	Supports another's sug-gestion	Compliments another	Puts down another	Gets another to talk

Based on your observations, answer the following:

List the status you observed you observe. Make up names for them.
Describes the roles that go with the statuses:

Statuses	Describe Roles

Is this a group, aggregate, or category?

Is this a formal or informal group?

Is this a primary or secondary group?

Chapter 13
Group Size

Background

Simmel (1950) first indicated that group size makes a difference in dynamics and balance of power. He compares dyads with triads and distinguishes them from larger groups. More recently, Kanter (1977) shows how proportions within groups also affect the treatment of minorities.

Objectives

Students participate in and compare different sized groups to experience participant observation and also group dynamics.

Topics

Groups

Gender

Minorities

Participant Observation

Materials required

None

To prepare

Decide a topic that students can discuss, where they might have different opinions. Examples include current events in the news such as a trial or something about a famous person.

Optional: Assign students to read selections from Simmel, Kanter or a text book chapter on groups.

Steps:

1. Explain that you are going to divide the class into different-sized groups to discuss something. They need to do two things at the same time:
   - Discuss the topic
   - Observe the group

2. Divide the class into at least one of each of the following:
   - Dyad, some mixed gender, some single gender
   - Triads, some mixed gender, some single gender
   - Small group (5-7 people), some mixed gender, some single gender
   - Larger group - up to 20 people

3. Tell them the topic, possibly write the topic as well.

4. Tell them to start.

5. Stop them after 20 minutes or more.

6. Ask them to take notes on their observations.

7. Again divide the class into different-sized groups, this time so that each person participates in a different size group than before.

8. Give them the same or a different topic.

9. Get them started.

10. Stop after 20 minutes and ask them to take notes on what differences they observed.

Discuss

1. Discuss their observations about size. "What were the main differences you observed among the groups in which you participated?" List dyad, triad, small group, larger group in columns on a board, chart or overhead. What are distinguishing characteristics or hypotheses about each size of group?

2. Discuss their observations about proportions. Ask if one gender talked more or controlled the group more. How did the numbers, the proportion of minorities or gender distinctions make a difference?

3. How do your findings relate to Simmel, Kanter or other group theories?

Problem-Solve

Problem

Group doesn't talk, no one says anything.

Solution

Ask the group a question or make a comment to get them started.

Problem

Group gets off on a different topic.

Solution

In the discussion, make use of this and ask how it happened. Would it just happen in certain size groups or certain group proportions?

Chapter 14

Culture

Background

    Culture, which includes values, language and customs, all of which unite and distinguish groups of people, is one of the major divisions of sociology and anthropology. Field work informs social scientists about specific aspects of culture. A film or video of a different culture can approximate field work, even if in a cursory way.

Objectives

    Students identify aspects of culture from a film or video.

    Students distinguish culture from social structure and other sociological topics.

Topics

    Culture

    Field work

Materials required

    Film or video of a different culture, such as those by National Geographic, the Yanomamo, or even excepts from the movie, *The Gods must be Crazy.*

To Prepare

    Assign students reading on culture and/or lecture on culture before this exercise.

    If desired, purchase a candy bar or some other kind of prize.

Steps:

1. Explain that you are going to show a video about a different culture. Students should list each cultural happening that they observe, for example, the click sound which the Bushmen make. (Optional) The one with the longest list wins a prize.

2. Show the video.

Discuss

1. Ask several students to tell what is on their list as you write on the board.

2. (Optional) Ask who had the most and ask that person to read all on her list.

3. What different categories of culture do we see on the list, for example, tools, traditions, or trade patterns?

4. What is culture?

5. How does the video relate to other ideas the class has discussed about culture?

Problem-solve

Problem

Student can't find any culture in the video.

Solution

Find out the reason the student is having difficulty. Maybe the student doesn't understand the concept of culture and may need help outside of class.

Problem

Students' lists vary.

Solution

Some students will find more aspects of culture than others. That's how they can learn from one another. This exercise could also involve small groups to share and compare answers.

Chapter 15

Cultural Exchange

Background

Studying another culture opens students eyes to their own culture. Students start to see that much of their every day life has patterns that contribute to American culture. Awareness of their own culture solidifies when students must explain and present something about their culture as if to foreign strangers.

If you want a structured simulation, Shirts (1973) and Eden and Last (1982) offer games, BaFa BaFa and Sumah. The game Hierophant's Heaven (Kohn and Kent 1984) lets students experience different religious beliefs. See also Barnak (1979) and Holmes and Guild (1979) for role plays relevant to cultural differences. Junn (1994) devised a situation where students experience communication problems with a different language.

Objectives

Students present examples of their own culture to demonstrate their understanding of culture and their understanding of the differences among cultural groups.

When to use

After extensive study of a different culture.

Topics

Culture

Materials required

None, unless students themselves want to bring in artifacts, music or other indicators of culture.

To Prepare

> Students should previously have read a monograph, such as *The Tiwi of North Australia* (Hart, Pilling and Goodale, 1988), or some other readings that inform them in-depth of a culture different from their own.

Steps:

1. Explain that students as groups will decide and present something of their own culture, as if to the members of the other culture they studied. For example, students might explain washing hands before they eat, bring in soap and towels, show pictures of sinks. Encourage them to review what they know about the other culture and find equivalents. Suggest that the culture could be their age group, their geographical region or the nation.

2. Divide the class into small groups of 5-7 people per group.

3. Give them most of a class period to choose a cultural topic and how they will present it. Usually, students want time outside of class to bring in items.

4. At the next class period, ask each group to present their cultural topic.

Discuss

1. What are differences between our culture and the one we studied?

2. What is culture?

3. Which part of culture did we see in the class presentations?

Problem-solve

Problem

> Students can't think of anything.

Solution

First ask them about the other culture, such as, "What do people do there on a daily basis? What are special occasions and what do they do then? Do you have anything like that?"

If that doesn't work, suggest music, dance, customs, food and other topics.

Problem

Different groups present the same cultural item.

Solution

Discuss with the whole class why this might have happened. Is that item more prevalent in our culture?

Chapter 16
Debates

Background

Most sociological theories and ideas have proponents and opponents. Students often feel strongly about certain topics. Debates hone skills in arguing for an opinion and critical thinking in evaluating others' arguments. Green and Klug (1990) show how they used debates in class and improved test performances.

Objectives

Students present evidence that supports one side of an argument, criticize others' arguments and answer criticisms about others' arguments.

Topics

Religion

Politics

Economics

Values

Education

Crime, for example, Capital Punishment, Gun Control

Deviance

Rural-Urban Differences (the example given here)

Materials required

None

To prepare

    1. Choose a topic, narrow or broad.

    2. Decide whether all of the class or selected members will debate; whether the debate will be spontaneous or whether you want them to prepare.

Steps:

    1. Explain that the class is going to have a debate on rural-urban differences. One side will make a point about the benefit of one or the other place, for example a greater variety of stores in cities. The other side will answer. The original side then can reply. Then the second side makes a point about their location. Continue until everyone has had a chance to answer.

    2. Divide the class in half. Ask all those sitting to the left of the center to line up against the wall. Ask all those sitting to the right of center to line up against the windows.

    3. Designate one side rural and one side urban. (Optional) Give students a chance to cross to a different side if they prefer.

    4. Ask for a volunteer to start, or start with the first student in line. For example, "What does a city have that a rural area does not?" or "What's one benefit of living in a rural area instead of a city?"

    5. Ask the first student on the other side to answer or refute what the first student said.

    6. Ask the second student on the first side to counter-argue. Encourage students to give specific evidence.

    7. Continue until all students have answered at least once and most points are exhausted.

Discuss

    1. What do you conclude from this discussion?

2. Has anyone changed an opinion or been convinced by the opposite side?

3. How does this discussion relate to readings? (for example, Wirth, Simmel, Toennies, Suttles)

Problem-solve

Problem

Students want to jump to a different point instead of answering or refuting a point.

Solution

Referee the debate and bring students back to the point originally raised.

Problem

Students who have nothing to say or don't have answers.

Solution

Refer them to reading pages, give them time to think. Ask their team-mates to confer with them and advise them what to say.

Chapter 17

Draw a Picture

Background

Symbols and pictures can encompass a number of topics. Not only
are they more right-brained activities, but they communicate a lot in
a small space. For many topics, students can draw a picture to unite
and compress their ideas and understanding of concepts.

Objectives

Students draw a picture or symbol of a Japanese corporation to
contrast with United States corporations.

Topics

Organizations

Social Structure

Economic Institutions

Bureaucracies

Materials required

None

To Prepare

- If applicable, assign readings on the topic, in this case, United
  States and Japanese corporations.

- Decide the topic to be drawn and whether the drawing project is
  with individuals or groups.

Steps:

1. Explain that the assignment is to symbolize or draw a Japanese
   corporation. For example, if you draw a United States corporation, it

would tend to be pyramidal, with a boss and owners on top, then various levels down to laborers. Your picture should show how Japanese corporations differ from United States corporations.

2. Divide the class into groups of 5-6 people per group.

3. Give them 20-30 minutes to discuss ideas.

4. Call on groups to draw their pictures on the board.

5. Ask each to give a brief explanation of how to view the symbol.

Discuss

1. What do the drawings in the class have in common?

2. Are there other aspects of Japanese corporations that they couldn't draw?

3. What are the major differences between U.S. corporations and Japanese corporations?

Problem-solve

Problem

Students can't figure out ideas.

Solution

Ask them to draw anything to get started on ideas. Ask, what are characteristics of Japanese corporations? How could you represent that?

Problem

Students complain they can't draw.

Solution

Advise them to sketch shapes or use something like stick figures.

Chapter 18

Family Decisions

Background

One of the ways to understand family dynamics and theories is to act like families. Although students participate in their own families, when they take other roles and participate in a more self-conscious way, they realize many of the ideas from textbooks.

Structured games such as The Marriage Game (Greenblat, Stein and Washburn 1977), Generation Gap (Boocock and Erling 1969), Soap Opera Game (Levinson 1980), CARS (Connection and Relationship Simulation) (Breci and Klein 1987) provide similar class activities.

Objectives

Students make family decisions to observe dynamics and changes in families over life cycles.

Topics

Marriage and Family

Materials required

None

Preparation

Assign readings on marriage and family.

Steps:

1. Give directions by telling students they will work with a partner as if they are a married or about to be married couple. Their job is to list all the items they need to decide at that stage of couplehood.

2. Pair up students and assign them to one of the following:

- couple considering marriage

- couple are engaged, have decided on marriage

- couple deciding whether to have children

- couple with young children

- couple with older children (teens)

- couple with children contemplating divorce

- couple without children contemplating divorce

- couple with aging parents

- aging couple

3. Get them started.

4. For larger classes, after couples have decided, group all those with the same life cycle stage to compare their decisions.

5. Ask each life cycle group to report.

Discuss

1. How did you know what topics to include?

2. How do couples make decisions on each of these topics?

3. What else do families need to decide?

4. What different structures of American families does this exercise show?

5. What other structures are there in the world?

6. How did your experience as a couple relate to the readings on families?

Problem-solve

Problem

Students can't think of anything.

Solution

Refer them back to the readings or get other students to help.

Chapter 19

Cooperation and Competition

Background

Children in the United States typically play competitive games and sports. Playing the same games in cooperative ways lets students see the differences between cooperation and competition. Cooperative and competitive issues have implications for the difference between capitalism and socialism as well as for education. Many children's games can be used; here we take the example of Blind Person's Bluff.

For a more structured game based on economic systems, see Cooperation (Bain 1984).

Objectives

Students play a game competitively.

Students play the same game cooperatively.

Topics

Societies - socialist and capitalist

Communities - communes

Education

Materials required

Blind fold

Steps:

1. Explain that as participant observers, students should experience the difference between playing games competitively and cooperatively. One person will be blind-folded in the middle of the group. The others must

remain in place in a circle around the blind-folded person while that person tries to identify the person he or she has touched.

2. Divide the class into groups of 10.

3. In each group, choose a person to be "it."

4. Blind fold the person and put her or him in the middle of the group.

5. Direct the blind-folded person to locate other people and guess who they are.

6. When the blind-folded person has guessed a person, that person becomes "it."

7. Repeat two to three times.

8. For the next round, ask the groups to be cooperative. Help the blind-folded person find another person. Give hints about who this person is.

9. Repeat two to three times.

Discuss

1. Which way did you prefer? Why?

2. How was it different for people in the circle? For the blind-folded person?

3. How could some competitive ways about our society be changed? What would be the outcome?

4. What are the benefits of competition? What harm does competition cause?

5. What are the pluses and minuses of cooperation?

Problem-solve

Problem

Some students may refuse to play.

Solution

Suggest that the non-players observe.

Chapter 20

Set Up A Corporation

Background

One of the most important United States social structures is the
corporation. When students jointly set up a corporation, they better
understand how corporations organize and the problems of any
institutions such as relations with other institutions, rules and
regulations, leadership and decision making.

You can also purchase games with more specific and elaborate
directions. In CLUG (Community Land Use Game) (Feldt 1972),
players create a construction company while The Commons game
(Powers 1987) challenges players to see the trade-offs between
individual gain and the collective good. Simsoc (Gamson 1978) and
They Shoot Marbles, Don't They? (Goodman 1974) let participants
build societies. All of these require several hours, and SimSoc
requires a whole semester.

Objectives

Students devise a corporation to understand how institutions work.

Topics

Organizations

Social Structure

Economic Institutions

Bureaucracies

Materials required

None

To Prepare

- Assign readings or lectures on institutions.

- This activity could be open-ended, based entirely on the
  students' creativity or you could set up a scenario for them of
  resources, needs, availability and other items.

Steps:

1. Explain that students will be in groups to set up a corporation. They are
   to decide a product, what resources they need, how they will organize,
   what their goal or mission is, and what they need to do first.

2. Divide them into groups of 5-7 people.

3. Allow at least 50 minutes.

4. Ask each group to report on what they will do.

Discuss

1. As each group reports, ask for feedback and ideas from others.

2. What do you conclude about how corporations form?

3. What are problems with the organization of corporations?

4. What other institutions relate to corporations? How did you deal with
   inputs and outputs?

5. How does this relate to readings/lectures?

Problem-solve

Problem

Students can't think of an idea for a corporation.

Solution

Ask them, What are your interests? Based on their interests, assign a
product, such as the generic widgets, or ask them to set up a music
recording studio or a company that promotes comedians or a
restaurant.

Chapter 21

Mapping

Background

Gerald Suttles (1972) suggests that each community member carries a slightly different view of their community, the space to which they feel a sense of belonging. He calls this cognitive mapping. Stoneall (1983) carried out research that asked various community members to draw a map of their community. The differences among them allowed her to analyze the range of borders of the community and gender differences in the perception of community.

Objectives

Students draw a map of their communities.

Topics

Community

Urban

Materials required

Blank sheets of paper

Preparation

Optional - Assign readings on communities.

Steps:

1. Explain that students are going to draw maps of what they consider their communities in order to analyze them and get a variety of views of the extent and content of communities.

2. Ask students to draw a map of their community.

3. Divide the class into groups of 5-8 students, possibly by students who live in the same community.

4. Ask the groups to analyze the maps and determine what they have in common. What is the range of borders and extent of communities? What kinds of things are shown on the map? (names, streets, buildings, other pictures)

Discuss

1. What was the smallest size of community? What was the largest?

2. What kind of symbols or icons did maps have? Which ones were on all the maps?

3. What variables do you relate to the categories? (rural-urban, size of community, gender differences)

4. How do your findings compare to what you have read about communities?

Problem-solve

Problem

Students complain they can't draw to scale or in correct perspective.

Solution

Reassure them that's okay.

Problem

Students draw "wrong," such as put the south at the top.

Solution

Show the class that it isn't wrong, but a source of data that tells something about the community members and their relation to the community.

Chapter 22

Prisoners and Guards

Background

In the early 1970s, Zimbardo (1972) and colleagues set up a fake prison in a Stanford University basement. They advertised for students and paid the 70 recruits as experimental subjects who were randomly assigned as prisoners and guards. Zimbardo's team locked up the prisoners, and the guards worked in three hour shifts. The experiment, meant to last for two weeks, actually ended after six days because the researchers were so disturbed at what they saw. They found the prisoners so easily became like prisoners and gave up and acted docile and institutionalized. Even worse were the guards. About one-third of the guards were tyrannical and made and enacted harsh rules. The other guards did favors for the prisoners, but none of them tried to stop the tyrannical guards.

With only one hour periods and not an actual lock-up, when students role-play prisoners and guards, some of the same issues appear.

Objectives

Students role-play prisoners and guards to see how the prison situation influences behaviors and attitudes.

Topics

Criminology

Deviance

Social Problems

Materials required

None

To Prepare
Steps:

1. Divide the class into two groups, with one-fifth of the class as guards.

2. Designate one group as prisoners and the others as guards.

3. Separate the prisoners into pairs or trios in different parts of the room.

4. Gather the guards and tell them to devise rules for what to do with the prisoners.

5. Direct the guards to carry out their rules.

Discuss

1. What did you think and feel as a prisoner?

2. What did it make you prisoners want to do?

3. What did you think and feel as a guard?

4. What did it make you guards want to do?

5. What did you notice about the rules? How did they resemble real prison rules? What's the purpose of the rules?

6. What differences did you notice among the guards? Why did they act that way? How does this relate to corruption?

7. Should prisons be for control, for punishment or for rehabilitation? Which did this experiment show?

Problem-solve

Problem

- Guards enact harsh, unrealistic rules.

- Students rebel and refuse to be either prisoners or guards.

- Prisoners escape and leave class.

Solution

All these fit what Zimbardo discovered. They also indicate

something about prisons and the prisoner-guard relationship.

Chapter 23

Consciousness-Raising

Background

Feminism borrowed the idea of consciousness raising from revolutionary groups that advocated telling one another the wrongs committed against them. This way, each would see they weren't alone in the injustices suffered and others would realize the greater extent of problems. Consciousness raising was an early step towards fighting against social injustice. Before people could fight, they had to understand that a problem existed.

Objectives

Students participate in consciousness-raising groups to understand how oppressed people discussed problems.

Topics

Gender

Race

Discrimination

Social Movements

Revolutions

Groups

Materials required

None

To Prepare

Decide the topic of the consciousness raising and how many groups you will have. The example below relates to women's and men's movements.

Steps:

1. Explain that the class is going to try out consciousness raising to see what it's like. They should take turns talking about something that's happened to them as a woman or man which they felt was unfair. For example, a teacher called some class members "men" and other class members "girls". Other group members are supposed to listen, be supportive and not evaluate or condemn.

2. Divide the class into one group (or more) with all women and another with all men. Ideally, the groups should have no more than 15 members.

3. Get the groups going. If necessary, call on one person to start and have them go around their circle.

4. At the end of the period or at the next period, discuss their experience.

Discuss

1. What themes came out of the groups? List the topics for men and women separately.

2. What was it like to participate in a group like that? Relate their experiences to women's movements or other actionable groups.

3. What differences can we conclude from the two groups?

4. Why are there differences?

5. What differences did you notice between the experience here and the readings about the Suffragette Movement (or other movements)?

6. What historical factors contribute to the differences?

Problem-solve

Problem

Students feel it's too personal and they don't want to talk.

Solution

Assign those students as observers to draw conclusions from the discussion.

Problem

Students don't see any gender problems within themselves.

Solution

Ask those students to listen and see if they can relate to what others say.

Chapter 24

Brown Eyes-Blue Eyes

Background

In 1968 when Martin Luther King was assassinated, Jane Elliott a teacher in a small town in Iowa, decided to provide her grade school class with first hand experience of discrimination, rather than just talk about the death. She treated brown-eyed children differently than blue-eyed children, and they responded accordingly. She also reversed the situation in whom she mistreated, and the same thing happened.

Simulation games can give similar experiences. In the Thorpe Game (Oxman 1983), players experience inequity in education. Junn (1994) also mentions a game where students each have a label on their backs of a type of person such as white sorority woman or African American male athlete. As students mingle they respond to the labeled students accordingly. Then students guess their label.

Objectives

Students experience discrimination and differential treatment to draw conclusions about theories of minorities and to have an idea of what daily life is like for minorities.

When to use

Use this activity over one or more class periods in conjunction with discussions or other activities that require you to call on students.

Topics

Discrimination and prejudice

Race and ethnicity

Class and stratification

Gender

Materials required

None

Optional materials

Treats for the favored group such as candy

To Prepare

- Decide a category for dividing the class into two sections. In addition to eye color, you could use month of birth, home town, initials.

- Decide which group you will harass.

Note: It helps make the point to favor the group whose characteristics you share and to harass the ones who are opposite to you.

For example, if you have brown eyes, favor the brown-eyed students and discriminate against those who have blue eyes.

- You may want to have the students switch places and repeat the exercise with the roles reversed.

Steps:

1. Announce you are going to conduct an experiment in class.

2. Ask all the blue-eyed students to sit in the back of the room and the brown-eyed students to sit in the front because they're better.

3. Ask the blue-eyed students to move even further back so the rest of us don't have to be too near to them.

4. Make disparaging remarks about the blue-eyes in third person terms, such as,

   "We feel sorry for them."

   "They can't help the way they are."

   "They aren't very healthy."

   "They smell bad because they aren't very clean."

   "They aren't very smart."

   "They don't know better."

   "We can't trust them. They might try to steal from us or even harm the rest of us."

5. Praise the brown-eyed students and offer them comfort or even treats. Use first or second person.

   "You're the really smart ones."

   "You can understand better than those others."

   "The best looking and most successful people have brown eyes."

   "You know all the answers."

6. Proceed with the lecture, discussion or other activity. Avoid eye contact with the blue-eyed students and do not call on them when they raise their hands. Continue to put down the blue-eyed students and praise the brown-eyed students. Even call on some brown-eyed students who do not raise their hands and tell them, "I know you know this."

7. Give the brown-eyed students extra privileges such as leaving first. Make the blue-eyed students do manual work such as pick up litter in the class or clean the board.

Discuss

Discuss the activity during the next class or at the end of the class experiment. Remind them that it was an experiment and that you really don't believe what you said against blue-eyed students.

1. Blue-eyed students, what did you think was happening? How did you feel?

2. Brown-eyed students, what did you think was happening? How did you feel?

3. How can we compare what happened in class with what happens in society?

4. How does the experiment relate to readings on discrimination?

Problem-solve

Problem

Students in the back may revert to child-like, disruptive behavior.

Solution

Treat them as children. Point out to the others how this shows their inferior nature.

In the discussion, ask what would happen to such children? They would be taken out of class, maybe even suspended. How does that lower their educational attainment?

Problem

Some students might not fit either category, such as green-eyed students.

Solution

Choose one of the following suggestions:

• Ask them to choose a group.

- Make them an additional group that is neutral; neither praise nor disapprove them.
- Designate them as observers.

Problem

Students may go over to another side.

Solution

Ask the students in that category to decide what to do. In the discussion, ask what happens to people who try to "pass?"

Problem

The harassed group pays no attention and some of them miss the discussion points.

Solution

- Make a point of discussing why some people may not do well in school, may not like school enough to continue.
- Help those students get the information they may have missed because of the experiment.

Chapter 25

Jeopardy Review

Background

Jeopardy is a television game show that most students have seen.
Playing it can be a fun way to review definitions. See Grauerholz,
(1991) and Kowalewski (1985) for alternative ways to use quiz
show formats. In this game, students receive an answer, and they
must make up a question. The answers can be examples, definitions
or concepts themselves.

Objectives

Students state a definition or a concept as a way to review.

Topics

Any topic

Materials required

Score keeping mechanism - a blackboard will do.

Optional materials

Jeopardy music

Fancy holders for different values of questions.

Bells or dingers

Prizes

To Prepare

Answers to questions - based on material covered for a test.

Assignment of variable points or dollar amounts to different
answers.

Steps:

1. Explain that students will play Jeopardy to review. Tell them the topics and the values within each topic.

2. Divide the class into two teams or into multiple teams that take turns, up to ten members per team. Team members take turns coming up with the question, although other team members can help them. Each team must signal when they know the question - either with bell or dinger or calling out or knocking on the table/desk.

3. Let the first team choose a topic and a value.

4. Give the answer.

5. The first team that signals can give a question. They then choose the next topic and value.

6. If that team has the question wrong, call on another team.

7. Continue until all answers have questions.

8. For the bonus point, give a harder answer and each team bids a certain amount and writes a question.

9. The team with the most points wins.

Problem-solve

Problem

Not everyone gets a chance to ask a question.

Solution

Listeners can sill benefit somewhat from hearing answers and questions and preparing to answer.

As an alternative, some teams can state the answers.

Problem

Two or more simultaneously signal to state question.

Solution

Ask other teams to decide or give another answer.

Bibliography

Adorno, T.W. *The Authoritarian Personality*. New York: Harper, 1950.

American Sociology Association. "Preface." *Liberal Learning and the Sociology Major: A Report to the Profession*. Washington: American Sociological Association, 1991.

Aronson, E. *The Jigsaw Classroom*. Newbury Park, California: Sage, 1978.

Astin, A.W. *What Matters in College? Four Critical Years*. San Francisco: Jossey-Bass, 1992.

_____. *Achieving Educational Excellence*. San Francisco: Jossey-Bass, 1985a.

_____. "Student Involvement: A Developmental Theory for Higher Education." *Journal of College Student Personnel*. July (1985): 297-308.

Bain, Robert. "Cooperation: The Wealth of Nation's Game." New York: Gelber Marketing, 1984.

Bales, Robert. *Interaction Process Analysis: A Method for the Study of Small Groups*. Cambridge: Addison-Wesley, 1966.

Barnak, P. "Role-Playing." In *Intercultural Sourcebook: Cross-Cultural Training Methodologies*, edited by D. S. Hoopes and P. Ventura, pp. 7-10. Washington, D.C.: Intercultural Network, 1979.

Bateman, Walter. *Open to Question*. San Francisco: Jossey-Bass, 1990.

Billison, Janet. "The College Classroom as a Small Group." *Teaching Sociology* 14 (1986): 143-151.

Boocock, Sarane, and Schild, Erling. "The Generation-Gap (Parent-Child Game)." Indianapolis: Bobbs-Merrill, 1969.

Breci, Michael, and Klein, Ross. "Communication and Relationship Simulation (CARS): A Reality-Based Means for Teaching Courtship, Marriage and the Family." *Teaching Sociology* 15 (1987): 285-91.

Brophy, J., and Good, T. "Teacher Behavior and Student Achievement." In *Handbook of Research on Teaching*, edited by M. Wittrock, pp. 328-375. New York: Macmillan, 1986.

Bryjak, George, and Soroka, Michael. *Sociology: Cultural Diversity in a Changing World.* Needham Heights, Massachusetts: Allyn and Bacon, 1994.

Cooper, James; Robinson, Pamela; and McKinney, Molly. "Cooperative Learning in the Classroom," In *Changing College Classrooms: New Teaching and Learning Strategies for an Increasingly Complex World,* edited by Diane Halpern, pp. 74-92. San Francisco: Jossey-Bass, 1994.

Dewey, John. *Experience and Education.* New York; Macmillan, 1947.

Dillon, J. T. *Questioning and Teaching: A Manual of Practice.* New York: Teachers College Press, 1988.

Dorn, Dean. "The First Day of Class: Problems and Strategies." *Teaching Sociology* 15 (1987): 61-72.

———. "Simulation Games. *Teaching Sociology*: 17 (1989): 1 -18.

Durkheim, Emile. *Suicide: A Study in Sociology*, translated by John Spaulding and Geoge Simpson. Glencoe: Free Press, 1951.

Eden, Tina, and Last, John. "Sumah: An Intercultural Game." Brighton UK: Brighton Polytechnic, Department of Visual Communication, 1982.

Forbess-Greene, Sue. *Encyclopedia of Ice Breakers.* San Diego: Pfeiffer, 1983.

Feldt, Alan. "CLUG-Community Land Use Game." New York: Macmillan, The Free Press, 1972.

Gamson, William. "Simsoc: Simulated Society." New York: Macmillan, The Free Press, 1978.

Garfinkel, Harold. *Studies in Ethnomethodology*. Englewood Cliffs, New Jersey: Prentice Hall, 1967.

Goffman, Erving. *The Presentation of Self in Everyday Life*. New York: Doubleday, 1959.

_____. *Gender Advertisements*. New York: Harper and Row, 1979.

Goodman, Fred. "They Shoot Marbles Don't They?" Asheville, N.C.: National Gaming Center, University of North Carolina, 1974.

Grauerholz, Elizabeth. "This is Jeopardy: How to Make Preparation for Exams Fun and Challenging." *Teaching Sociology* 19 (1991): 495-97.

Green, Charles, and Klug, Hadley. "Teaching Critical Thinking and Writing Through Debates: An Experimental Evaluation." *Teaching Sociology* 18 (1990): 462-471.

Greenblat, Cathy; Stein, Peter; and Washburne, Norman. "The Marriage Game." New Brunswick, New Jersey: Rutgers University, 1977.

Hamlin, John, and Janssen, Susan. "Active Learning in Large Introductory Sociology Courses." *Teaching Sociology* 15 (1987): 45-54.

Hansen, C. Bobbi. "Questioning Techniques for the Active Classroom, " In *Changing College Classrooms: New Teaching and Learning Strategies for an Increasingly Complex World*, edited by Diane Halpern, pp. 93-106. San Francisco: Jossey-Bass, 1994.

Hart, C.W.M.; Pilling, Arnold; and Goodale, Jane. The *Tiwi of North Australia,* Third Edition. New York: Holt, Rinehart, Winston, 1988.

Holmes, H., and Guild, S. "Role-Plays," In *Intercultural Sourcebook: Cross-Cultural Training Methodologies,* edited by D.S. Hoopes and P. Ventura, pp. 11-14. Washington, D.C.: Intercultural Network, 1979.

Ingalesbee, Timothy. "Conceive a Community: A Group Exercise for Teaching the Theory and Practice of Communitarianism." *Teaching Sociology* 20 (1992): 294-301.

Inbar, Michael, and Stoll, Clarice. *Simulation and Gaming in Social Science*. New York: Free Press, 1972.

Johnson, David, and Johnson, Robert. *Cooperation and Competition: Theory and Research*. Edina, Minnesota: Interaction Book, 1989.

Johnson, David; Johnson, Robert; and Holubec, Edythe. *Circles of Learning*. Edina, Minnesota: Interaction Book, 1986.

Johnson, David; Johnson, Robert; and Smith, K.A. *Active Learning: Cooperation in the College Classroom*. Edina, Minnesota: Interaction Book, 1991.

Junn, Ellen. "Experiential Approaches to Enhancing Cultural Awareness." In *Changing College Classrooms: New Teaching and Learning Strategies for an Increasingly Complex World,* edited by Diane Halpern, pp. 128-164. San Francisco: Jossey-Bass, 1994.

Karp, David, and Yoels, William. "The College Classroom: Some Observations on the Meaning of Student Participation." *Sociology and Social Research* 60 (1976): 421-39.

Kanter, Rosabeth Moss. *Men and Women of the Corporation*. New York: Doubleday, 1977.

Keating, Barbara. "Reducing Classroom Alienation: Applications from Theory." *Teaching Sociology* 15 (1987) : 407-413.

King, Alison. "Inquiry as a Tool in Critical Thinking." In *Changing College Classrooms: New Teaching and Learning Strategies for an Increasingly Complex World,* edited by Diane Halpern, pp. 13-38. San Francisco: Jossey-Bass, 1994.

Kolb, David. *Experiential Learning: Experiences as the Source of Learning and Development*. Englewood Cliffs, N.J.: Prentice Hall, 1984.

Kohn, Rachel, and Kent, Stephen. "Hierophant's Heaven." Hamilton Ontario:

    Instructional Development Centre, McMaster University, 1984.

Kowalewski, David. "Reviewing for the Final: The Gameshow Technique." *Teaching

    Sociology* 14 (1985) 276-78.

Levinson, Richard. "The Soap Opera Game." *Teaching Sociology* 7 (1980):181-190.

Lewis, Linda, and Williams, Carol. "Experiential Learning Past and Present." *Experiential

    Learning: A New Approach.* Edited by Lewis Jackson and Rosemary Caffarella, pp.

    5-16. San Francisco: Jossey-Bass,1994.

McKinney, Kathleen, and Graham-Buxton, Mary. "The Use of Collaborative Learning

    Groups in the Large Class." *Teaching Sociology* 21 (1993): 403-8.

Mead, G.H. *Mind, Self and Society.* Chicago: University of Chicago Press, 1934.

Newstrom, John, and Scannell, Edward. *Games Trainers Play.* New York: McGraw Hill,

    1980.

_____. *Still More Games Trainers Play.* New York: McGraw Hill, 1991.

_____. *Even More Games Trainers Play.* New York: McGraw Hill, 1994 .

Oxman, Wendy. "The Thorp Game." Asheville, N.C.: National Gaming Center,

    University of North Carolina, 1983.

Plato. *Plato: The Collected Dialogues,* edited by Edith Hamilton and Huntington Cairns.

    New York: Pantheon Books, 1961.

Powers, Richard. "The Commons Game: The Relation Between Scarce Resources and

    Interdependence." Asheville, N.C.: National Gaming Center, University of North

    Carolina, 1987.

Rau, William, and Heyl, Barbara Sherman. "Humanizing the College Classroom:

    Collaborative Learning and Social Organization Among Students." *Teaching

    Sociology* 18 (1990): 140-144.

Resnick, L. *Education and Learning to Think*. Washington, D.C.: National Academy
    Press, 1987.

Riffer, R.L. "The First Class: An Exercise for Introductory Sociology." *Teaching
    Sociology* 10 (1983): 262-265.

Scheff, Thomas. "Discovering Sociology." *Teaching Sociology* 20(1992): 248-53.

Shirts, Garry. "Starpower." Delmar, CA.: Simulation Training Systems, 1969.

_____. "BAFA BAFA." Delmar, CA.: Simulation Training Systems, 1973.

Slaven, R.E. "When Does Cooperative Learning Increase Student Achievement?"
    Psychological Bulletin 94 (1983): 429-445.

Stoneall, Linda. "Cognitive Mapping: Gender Differences in the Perception of
    Communities." *Sociological Inquiry* 51 (1983): 121-127.

_____. *How to Write Training Materials*. San Diego: Pfeiffer and Associates, 1991a.

_____. "Inquiring Trainers Want to Know." *Training and Development* (November,
    1991): 31-39.

Suttles, Gerald. *The Social Order of the Slum*. Chicago: University of Chicago Press,
    1972.

Tannen, Deborah. *You Just Don't Understand: Women and Men in Conversation*. New
    York: William Morrow, 1990.

Toll, Dove. "Ghetto." New York: Western, 1969.

Wilen, W.W., and Clegg, A. "Effective Questions and Questioning: A Research Review."
    Theory and Research in Social Education, 14 (1986): 153-161.

Zimbardo, Phillip. "The Pathology of Imprisonment." *Society* 9 (1972): 4-8.

Exercises Applicable to Allyn and Bacon Texts

Numbers refer to chapters.

Exercise	Henslin: Sociology	Hess/ Markson/ Stein: Sociology	Henslin: Essentials of Sociology	Eitzen/Baca Zinn: In Conflict and Order	Sullivan: Sociology	Bryjak/ Soroka: Sociology	Kammeyer/ Ritzer/ Yetman: Sociology
Break a Norm	2, 4	3, 4	2, 4	2	2, 4	2	3, 4
Scientific Problem	5	2				1	2
Take a Survey; Authori- tarian Personality	5, 15	2, 14	1, 9	14	13	1, 11	2, 16
Write a Survey; Religion	5, 18,	2, 16	1, 13	17	11	1, 10	2, 15
Interviews: Education	5	2, 15	13	16	12	1, 10	2, 12
Content Analysis: Gender	5, 11	2, 10	10	12	8	1, 7	2, 10
Library Research; Uniform Crime Report	5, 8	2, 17	6	7	5	1, 8	2, 6
Role Play; Theories	4, 1	5, 1	1	1	1	1	1
Impression Manage- ment	4	5	4			1, 3	4
Group Dynamics	4	4	5	2	4	3	4
Group Size	4	4	5	2	4	3	4
Culture	2	3	2	5	2	2	3
Cultural Exchange	2	3	2	5	2	2	3
Debates; Rural- Urban	20	21	13		14	13	17
Draw a Picture; Corpora- tions	4, 7, 9, 14	13	11	13	13	11	13
Family Decisions	16	12	12	15	9	9	11

Cooperation and Competition	9	3		4			
Set Up a Corporation	14	13	11	13	13	11	13
Mapping	20	21	14		14	13	17
Prisoners and Guards	8	17	6	7	5	8	6
Consciousness-Raising	11, 12, 13	10. 11	9, 10	11, 12	8, 7	7, 6	10, 9
Brown Eyes-Blue Eyes	12	11	9	11	7	6	9
Jeopardy Review	1-22	1-23	1-15	1-17	1-15	1-14	1-18

NOTES

NOTES

NOTES

NOTES